# DAILY JOY

## Discover Contentment, Peace, Purpose, and Growth for a Happiness Journey

### DILIP PATIL

## Copyright © 2024 by Dilip Patil

All rights reserved. No part of this book may be reproduced in any form without permission in writing from the author.

No part of this publication may be reproduced or transmitted in any form or by any means, mechanical or electronic, including photocopying or recording, information storage and retrieval system, email, or any other means, without permission in writing from the author.

## DEDICATION

This book is lovingly dedicated to my family—my unwavering foundation and guiding light. Your endless support and belief in me have fueled my journey of personal growth and have been the cornerstone in bringing this book to life. Your influence resonates in every word written and every lesson shared. Thank you for being my inspiration, my strength, and my home.

## YOUR GIFT: "THE SUCCESS FORMULA"

Thank you for joining me with **"DAILY JOY."** As a token of appreciation, I'm excited to offer you a complimentary copy of my eBook, "The Success Formula." This guide has insights and strategies to propel you further on your path to success.

"The Success Formula" complements the principles explored in **"DAILY JOY**," providing actionable steps for achieving goals and enhancing one's life. To download your free copy, click the link below or scan the QR code:

This eBook is my way of saying thank you and supporting you in your journey toward success and happiness.

Best wishes,

Dilip Patil

# TABLE OF CONTENTS

**INTRODUCTION** .................................................................... 6
    IMPORTANCE OF JOY IN EVERYDAY LIFE ................................. 7
    HOW JOY INFLUENCES OVERALL WELL-BEING AND PRODUCTIVITY ........ 8
    STORIES AND EXAMPLES ILLUSTRATING THE IMPACT OF JOY ........... 10
    BOOK'S STRUCTURE AND OBJECTIVES ................................... 12

**1   UNDERSTANDING JOY** ................................................ 16
    1.1   JOY VS. HAPPINESS ................................................ 16
    1.2   JOY'S BENEFITS ON HEALTH .................................... 18

**2   DISCOVERING CONTENTMENT** ................................. 22
    2.1   WHAT IS CONTENTMENT? ........................................ 23
    2.2   PRACTICES FOR CULTIVATING CONTENTMENT ............... 24

**3   FINDING INNER PEACE** ............................................ 27
    3.1   THE NATURE OF INNER PEACE .................................. 27
    3.2   INNER PEACE IN DAILY LIFE .................................... 32

**4   DEFINING YOUR PURPOSE** ...................................... 43
    4.1   IMPORTANCE OF PURPOSE ....................................... 43
    4.2   DISCOVERING YOUR PURPOSE .................................. 48

**5   EMBRACING PERSONAL GROWTH** ............................ 57
    5.1   THE JOURNEY OF GROWTH ...................................... 57
    5.2   STRATEGIES FOR PERSONAL GROWTH ....................... 62

**6   INTEGRATING JOY INTO DAILY LIFE** ........................ 69
    6.1   DAILY JOY PRACTICES ............................................. 69
    6.2   MAINTAINING JOY THROUGH CHALLENGES .................. 74

**7   CASE STUDIES AND PERSONAL STORIES** ................ 80
    7.1   REAL-LIFE EXAMPLES ............................................. 80
    7.2   REFLECTION AND APPLICATION ................................ 83

**8   THE BIGGER PICTURE** ............................................. 88
    8.1   JOY'S IMPACT ON THE WORLD .................................. 88

|      | 8.2  | Creating a Joyful Future ................................................... 92 |
| ---- | ---- | ---- |
| **9** | **CONCLUSION** ........................................................................ **98** | |
|      | 9.1  | Summarizing Key Takeaways ............................................... 98 |
|      | 9.2  | Highlights of the Most Important Lessons ..................... 100 |
| **10** | **APPENDICES** ..................................................................... **102** | |
|      | 10.1 | Daily Joy Journal Templates ........................................... 102 |
|      | 10.2 | Recommended Reading and Resources ........................... 104 |

**GRATITUDE AND ACKNOWLEDGEMENTS** ........................................ **108**

**YOUR FEEDBACK MATTERS** ............................................................ **110**

**ABOUT THE AUTHOR** ..................................................................... **112**

**EXPLORE MORE BOOKS** ................................................................. **114**

# INTRODUCTION

"Joy does not simply happen to us. We must choose joy and keep choosing it daily." – Henri J.M. Nouwen.

Welcome to "Daily Joy: Discover Contentment, Peace, Purpose, and Growth for a Happiness Journey," the first book of the series "HAPPINESS JOURNEY." Finding and nurturing joy in our daily lives can seem challenging in a world that often feels overwhelming and fast-paced. Our days are filled with endless tasks, responsibilities, and distractions that can leave us drained and disconnected from what truly matters. However, joy is not an elusive, distant goal but a tangible and transformative force we can cultivate with intention and practice. It's about discovering those small, everyday moments that spark joy and learning to appreciate them, no matter how hectic life becomes.

This book aims to guide you to discover and embrace joy in every aspect of your life, fostering a more profound sense of contentment, peace, and purpose. You will learn how to bring joy into your daily routines and mindset through thoughtful reflection, practical exercises, and real-life examples. By understanding the nature of joy and its profound impact on our well-being, you will be equipped with the tools to create a more joyful and fulfilling life. Whether you seek to improve your mental health, strengthen your relationships, or add happiness to your days, this journey will help you uncover and embrace the joy within you.

## IMPORTANCE OF JOY IN EVERYDAY LIFE

Joy is a fundamental aspect of the human experience, influencing our mental, emotional, and physical well-being. Unlike happiness, often tied to external circumstances, joy is an intrinsic state that can be nurtured through intentional practices and a positive mindset. It helps us navigate life's challenges with resilience and grace, offering a more profound sense of purpose and fulfillment.

Experiencing joy aligns us with our true selves, enriching our lives through simple, everyday moments and strengthening our connections with others. Joy is contagious, spreading positivity within our communities and fostering a greater sense of belonging. Moreover, it has tangible physical benefits, such as reducing stress and enhancing overall health, making us more vibrant participants in our own lives.

Understanding joy as both a choice and a practice empowers us to live more authentically and fully. By consciously cultivating joy, we can transform our lives and positively impact those around us, creating a ripple effect of well-being and connection.

## How Joy Influences Overall Well-Being and Productivity

Joy significantly impacts our mental and physical health. It reduces stress, enhances our immune system, and improves our resilience in facing challenges. When joyful, our productivity increases because we are more focused, motivated, and creative. Joy also fosters better relationships, as it helps us connect more deeply with others and build stronger, more supportive communities.

- **Mental Health Benefits:** Joy acts as a natural antidote to stress and anxiety by triggering the release of dopamine and serotonin, which lower cortisol levels and promote relaxation. This leads to improved mental clarity, mood, and cognitive function. Joy also enhances resilience, helping us recover from setbacks more quickly and view challenges as opportunities for growth. It fosters a balanced and positive mental state essential for overall well-being.
- **Physical Health Benefits:** Joy has significant physical health benefits, including a more robust immune system, lower blood pressure, and reduced risk of cardiovascular diseases, all due to

its stress-reducing effects. Joyful individuals are also more likely to make healthier lifestyle choices, such as exercising, eating well, and getting enough sleep, creating a positive feedback loop that enhances overall health and well-being.

- **Impact on Productivity:** Joy boosts productivity by fostering a positive, focused mindset that enhances engagement, creativity, and problem-solving. It helps us manage time effectively, reduces procrastination, and leads to proactive goal achievement, ultimately increasing personal and professional satisfaction.

- **Strengthening Relationships:** Joy strengthens relationships by radiating positivity and warmth, making us more approachable and fostering more profound connections. It encourages supportive and collaborative behaviors, creating a positive feedback loop that enhances mutual well-being and builds a robust and supportive community essential for emotional health.

Joy is a powerful force that enhances well-being and productivity. We can improve health, build resilience, boost productivity, and strengthen relationships by embracing joy.

## Stories and Examples Illustrating the Impact of Joy

Maya was a dedicated healthcare professional who often felt overwhelmed by the demands of her job. Working long hours in a high-stress environment took a toll on her mental and physical health. Determined to make a change, Maya started incorporating daily gratitude and mindfulness practices into her routine. Every morning, she spent a few minutes reflecting on what she was grateful for and setting positive intentions for the day. She also practiced mindful breathing exercises during her breaks to stay grounded. Over time, Maya noticed a significant improvement in her overall well-being. She felt more balanced, less stressed, and more connected to her purpose. This shift enhanced her mental health and made her more effective and compassionate in her interactions with patients and colleagues. Maya's newfound joy radiated outward, creating a more positive and supportive atmosphere at her workplace.

Another example is Alex, a high school teacher passionate about education but struggling with burnout. Determined to reignite his enthusiasm, Alex adopted joy-centered approaches in his classroom. He began each day with a brief mindfulness session, encouraging students to share something positive from their lives. He also integrated activities that fostered creativity and collaboration, making learning more enjoyable and engaging for his students. As a result, the classroom environment became more vibrant and upbeat. Students were more motivated, participation increased, and academic performance improved. Alex found that by prioritizing joy, not only did his students thrive, but he also rediscovered his passion for teaching and felt more fulfilled.

Then there's Priya, an entrepreneur juggling multiple responsibilities in her growing business. Feeling constantly stressed and disconnected from her family, Priya realized she needed to change. She started dedicating daily to activities that brought her joy, such as yoga, time in nature, and playing with her children. She also consciously practiced gratitude, writing down three things she was thankful for each night. These small changes had a profound impact on her life. Priya felt more energized, focused, and content. Her improved mental state positively influenced her business decisions, leading to better outcomes and growth. Moreover, her relationships with her family and team members strengthened, creating a more harmonious and productive environment at home and work.

These stories illustrate how prioritizing joy can lead to profound life changes. Individuals like Maya, Alex, and Priya transformed their experiences by integrating simple joy-centered practices, enhancing their well-being, productivity, and relationships. Their journeys highlight the tangible benefits of choosing joy and demonstrate that cultivating a joyful and fulfilling life is within everyone's reach.

## BOOK'S STRUCTURE AND OBJECTIVES

This book is structured to provide you with a comprehensive understanding of joy and practical strategies to incorporate it into your daily life. Each chapter focuses on a specific aspect of joy, guiding you through discovery, practice, and reflection. By breaking down the concept of joy into manageable and relatable sections, you can gradually integrate these principles into your everyday routines, leading to a more fulfilling and joyful life. Here's a detailed overview of the chapters:

1. **Understanding Joy:** This chapter lays the foundation by exploring what joy truly means. You will learn about the differences between joy and happiness and delve into the emotional aspects of joy. Additionally, we will discuss the scientific benefits of joy, supported by research findings that highlight its positive impact on mental and physical health.
2. **Discovering Contentment:** Contentment is critical to lasting joy. This chapter defines contentment and explains how it differs from

complacency. You will also discover various practices for cultivating contentment, such as mindfulness, gratitude journaling, and the power of acceptance and letting go.

3. **Finding Inner** peace is essential for sustaining joy. This chapter will help you understand its nature and how to achieve it daily. We will cover techniques such as meditation, creating a peaceful environment, and effectively managing stress and anxiety.

4. **Defining Your Purpose:** A sense of purpose greatly enhances our joy and fulfillment. Here, we will discuss the importance of having a purpose and share stories of purpose-driven lives. You will be guided through self-reflection exercises to discover your passions and strengths and learn how to set meaningful goals that align with your purpose.

5. **Embracing Personal Growth:** Personal growth is a continuous journey that fuels joy. This chapter will explain the differences between a growth mindset and a fixed mindset and highlight the benefits of personal development. You will explore strategies for learning new skills, seeking feedback, and overcoming the fear of failure.

6. **Integrating Joy into Daily Life:** Joy should be a part of your everyday routine. This chapter will discuss practical daily joy practices, including morning routines, finding joy in small moments, and building joyful habits. We will also address maintaining joy through challenges by coping with difficult times and building resilience.
7. **Case Studies and Personal Stories:** Real-life examples can be influential motivators. This chapter shares stories of individuals who have successfully found joy. These case studies provide valuable lessons and insights, and you will be encouraged to reflect on and apply these lessons to your own life through practical exercises.
8. **The Bigger Picture:** Joy extends beyond our personal lives. This chapter explores the broader impact of joy on the world and how living joyfully can influence others. You will learn about the ripple effect of joyful living and engage in visioning exercises to create a joyful future, making commitments to sustain joy in your life.

By reading this book, you will understand the nature of joy and how to cultivate it in your daily life. You will learn practical techniques to enhance your contentment, inner peace, purpose, and personal growth. The book provides a variety of exercises and reflections designed to help you internalize the concepts and apply them effectively. Through this journey, you will be equipped to:

- Recognize and appreciate the profound impact of joy on your well-being and productivity.
- Develop daily practices that nurture and sustain joy.
- Build resilience and maintain a positive mindset even in challenging times.
- Strengthen your relationships and contribute to a more joyful community.
- Envision and create a future filled with lasting joy.

This journey towards joy is an active and transformative process, inviting you to engage fully with the exercises and reflections in this book. By documenting your thoughts, revisiting the activities, and embracing joy as a daily choice, you will enhance your well-being and inspire those around you. Let's embark on this journey together, unlocking the profound impact of lasting joy on every aspect of your life.

# 1 UNDERSTANDING JOY

"Joy is the simplest form of gratitude." – Karl Barth.

Joy is a profound and multifaceted emotion that goes beyond mere happiness. It is a deep-seated sense of well-being that transcends external circumstances and is rooted in a positive mind. Understanding joy requires exploring its nature, differences from happiness, and emotional and scientific dimensions. This chapter will provide a comprehensive understanding of joy, setting the foundation for incorporating it into your daily life.

## 1.1 JOY VS. HAPPINESS

Understanding the difference between joy and happiness is essential for cultivating lasting well-being. Happiness is often linked to external events and circumstances, serving as a response to something pleasant or desirable. For instance, happiness might arise when you receive good news, indulge in a delicious meal, or achieve a significant goal. Because it is closely tied to external factors, happiness can be fleeting and temporary, disappearing as circumstances change.

Joy, in contrast, is a more profound and enduring state that is less dependent on what is happening around you. It is rooted in an internal sense of peace and contentment and is connected to an overall positive outlook on life. Joy can persist even in challenging times, providing a stable foundation that supports resilience and well-being.

To illustrate the difference, consider the example of receiving a promotion at work. Happiness might be the feeling of joy you experience upon hearing the news. Still, joy is the more profound satisfaction that comes from appreciating the journey and growth that led to that achievement. Similarly, happiness might come from a fun outing with friends, but joy is found in the lasting connections and shared memories you create with them. Joy goes beyond temporary pleasures and is embedded in the meaningful experiences and relationships that enrich our lives.

Joy is not a solitary emotion but is accompanied by many other positive emotions, such as gratitude, love, and contentment. These emotions significantly contribute to our overall well-being and sense of fulfillment. Experiencing joy can profoundly impact our outlook on life, fostering a more optimistic perspective that makes coping with stress and adversity easier.

One of joy's most significant emotional benefits is its role in building emotional resilience. Joy provides a stable foundation of positive feelings that help us recover from setbacks more quickly and maintain a balanced emotional state. This resilience is crucial in navigating life's inevitable ups and downs, allowing us to face challenges with greater confidence and composure.

People who experience joy regularly are often better equipped to handle life's difficulties and maintain a positive outlook, even in adversity. Joy buffers against negative emotions and stress, helping us remain grounded and centered. By cultivating joy, we can enhance our emotional resilience, leading to a more fulfilling and balanced life.

## 1.2 Joy's Benefits on Health

Experiencing joy has profound effects on both physical and mental health, making it a crucial component of a healthy lifestyle. Research shows joy can boost the immune system, making individuals less susceptible to illnesses. It encourages the production of antibodies and enhances the functioning of immune cells, which helps the body ward off infections and diseases more effectively.

Joy also contributes to cardiovascular health. Regular experiences of joy can lower blood pressure, reduce the risk of heart disease, and improve overall cardiovascular function. By reducing stress and promoting relaxation, joy helps maintain a healthy heart and circulatory system.

Additionally, joy reduces the levels of stress hormones, such as cortisol, in the body, leading to decreased anxiety and improved mental health. Lower cortisol levels help alleviate the harmful effects of chronic stress, promoting a state of calm and relaxation. Experiencing joy also increases the production of neurotransmitters like serotonin and dopamine, which are crucial for mood regulation and feelings of well-being. These chemicals play a significant role in enhancing our emotional resilience and overall happiness.

**Fundamental Studies and Their Implications**

Scientific studies have consistently shown that individuals who regularly experience joy tend to have longer life expectancies and better overall health. For instance, research conducted by the Harvard School of Public Health found a strong correlation between positive emotions and longevity. This study demonstrated that people who maintain a joyful outlook are more likely to live longer, healthier lives.

Another study from the University of California, Berkeley, highlighted that individuals who cultivate joy through practices like gratitude and mindfulness report higher levels of life satisfaction and lower levels of depression and anxiety. These findings suggest that joy is a fleeting emotion vital to a healthy and fulfilling life.

## Practical Applications of Research

The implications of these studies are clear: incorporating joy-inducing activities into your daily routine can have significant health benefits. Engaging in practices such as keeping a gratitude journal, participating in physical activities you enjoy, and spending quality time with loved ones can enhance your overall well-being. You can improve your mental and physical health by intentionally seeking joy and maintaining a positive mindset.

The science of joy underscores the importance of intentionally fostering joy in one's life. By prioritizing joyful experiences and adopting a positive outlook, one can create a foundation for lasting health and happiness.

Understanding joy's nature and benefits is the first step to integrating it into your life. By distinguishing joy from happiness and recognizing its emotional and health impacts, you're ready to pursue a more joyful existence. The following chapters will offer practical strategies to cultivate joy in your daily routine, leading to lasting fulfillment.

## 2 Discovering Contentment

*"Contentment is not the fulfillment of what you want, but the realization of how much you already have." – Anonymous.*

Contentment is a profound state where we find satisfaction and peace in the present moment, appreciating what we have rather than constantly striving for more. It involves a deep sense of inner fulfillment that comes from within, allowing us to feel complete and secure in our lives as they are. This internal state of contentment provides a stable foundation for enduring joy, enabling us to navigate life's ups and downs with grace and resilience.

Cultivating contentment can be a transformative practice that enhances our well-being in a world that often emphasizes acquisition and achievement. Unlike fleeting emotions tied to external events, contentment is a more lasting state that fosters a sense of balance and tranquility. Its enduring nature provides a sense of security and balance, allowing us to navigate life's challenges with grace and resilience. This chapter will delve into the true essence of contentment, exploring its differences from other emotional states, such as complacency and happiness, and offering practical guidance on how to nurture contentment in our daily lives. Understanding and embracing contentment can create a joy, gratitude, and peace-filled life.

## 2.1 WHAT IS CONTENTMENT?

Contentment is a state of inner peace and satisfaction that arises from appreciating what you have and where you are in life rather than constantly striving for more. It's not just about what you have but also about accepting and being at peace with your current situation. Unlike fleeting emotions like happiness, contentment is a stable and enduring state of being that isn't easily swayed by external circumstances. It involves a deep acceptance of the present moment and a recognition of the sufficiency of your current situation. Historically, contentment has been revered across cultures and philosophies as a key to living a fulfilling life. For example, Stoic philosophers valued contentment as a virtue of accepting life's circumstances with grace. At the same time, Eastern traditions like Buddhism emphasize contentment as a path to enlightenment through mindfulness and letting go of desires.

**Contentment vs. Complacency**

While contentment is a positive state of satisfaction, it can sometimes be confused with complacency—a state of self-satisfaction that leads to stagnation. Complacency involves a lack of desire to grow or improve, resulting in missed opportunities and failure to reach one's potential. On the other hand, healthy contentment allows for ambition and growth without the constant pressure of dissatisfaction. It's about finding a balance where you can appreciate your achievements and the present moment while pursuing goals and aspirations. Strategies to avoid complacency include setting personal and professional growth goals and regularly reflecting on your progress to ensure you're moving forward while maintaining a sense of satisfaction with where you are.

## 2.2 PRACTICES FOR CULTIVATING CONTENTMENT

Mindfulness is a powerful practice that helps cultivate contentment by keeping you grounded in the present moment. It involves paying attention to your thoughts, feelings, and surroundings without judgment. By practicing mindfulness daily, you can develop a deeper appreciation for life's simple pleasures and reduce the stress of dwelling on the past or worrying about the future. Techniques for practicing mindfulness include focused breathing exercises, mindful eating, and mindful walks. Real-life examples include setting aside a few minutes each morning to meditate or being fully present during a conversation, which can significantly enhance your contentment.

## Gratitude Journaling

Gratitude journaling is another effective practice for fostering contentment. It involves regularly writing down things you are grateful for, which shifts your focus from what you lack to what you have. This practice has been shown to improve mental health, increase happiness, and enhance overall well-being. To start a gratitude journal, set aside time each day to write down three things you are grateful for, no matter how small. Prompts such as "What made me smile today?" or "What am I thankful for in my relationships?" can guide your journaling. Over time, this practice can lead to a more content and positive outlook on life.

## Acceptance and Letting Go

Acceptance is a critical component of contentment, as it involves embracing life as it is rather than constantly yearning for it to be different. Letting go of negative thoughts and emotions, such as resentment or frustration, frees you from the mental burdens that hinder contentment. Techniques for acceptance and letting include cognitive reframing, challenging and changing negative thought patterns, and meditation practices that focus on releasing tension and negativity. Stories of individuals who have practiced acceptance often highlight how this approach has led to a greater sense of peace and contentment, even in challenging circumstances. Exercises such as writing down what you're holding onto and then consciously letting it go can be powerful tools for achieving a state of contentment.

Discovering contentment is about finding peace and satisfaction in the present moment, regardless of external circumstances. By understanding what contentment truly means and distinguishing it from complacency, you can cultivate this powerful state of being through mindfulness, gratitude journaling, and acceptance. These practices offer practical ways to integrate contentment into your daily life, helping you build a foundation of lasting happiness and well-being. As you continue your journey, remember that contentment is not about settling for less but about recognizing and appreciating the fullness of what you already have.

# 3 Finding Inner Peace

"Peace comes from within. Do not seek it without." – Buddha.

Inner peace is a serene state of mind that allows us to remain calm and centered, regardless of external circumstances. It is the foundation for mental and emotional well-being, enabling us to navigate life's challenges with grace and resilience. In this chapter, we will explore the nature of inner peace, its importance, and practical techniques to cultivate it in our daily lives.

## 3.1 The Nature of Inner Peace

Inner peace is a profound state of mental and emotional tranquility, marked by the absence of anxiety, stress, and worry. It involves a deep sense of calm, allowing us to navigate life's challenges with grace and resilience. Achieving inner peace means cultivating contentment and acceptance of the present moment, free from past regrets or future anxieties. This state is not just the absence of negative emotions but also the presence of positive qualities like patience, gratitude, and compassion. Embracing inner peace fosters a harmonious relationship with ourselves and our surroundings, helping us maintain balance and well-being in daily life.

**Characteristics of Inner Peace:** Inner peace is characterized by several distinct qualities contributing to a harmonious and balanced state of being. Here are some key characteristics:

1. **Calmness and Serenity:** Inner peace brings a sense of calmness and serenity not easily disturbed by external events. Individuals with inner peace remain composed and collected, even in stressful situations.
2. **Emotional Stability:** Those who experience inner peace exhibit emotional stability and resilience. They are less likely to be swayed by fluctuating emotions and can maintain a balanced state of mind.
3. **Acceptance:** Inner peace involves accepting life as it is without constantly striving to change or control everything. This acceptance includes acknowledging one's emotions and experiences without judgment.
4. **Clarity and Focus:** Individuals can think clearly and maintain focus with inner peace. Their minds are not cluttered with unnecessary worries, allowing them to make decisions with greater wisdom and insight.
5. **Presence in the Moment:** An essential aspect of inner peace is the ability to live in the present

moment. This mindfulness enables individuals to engage with their surroundings fully and appreciate the here and now.

6. **Compassion and Understanding:** Inner peace fosters compassion and understanding toward oneself and others. This quality enhances relationships and promotes a sense of interconnectedness.

7. **Gratitude:** Individuals with inner peace often express gratitude for their life circumstances, appreciating the simple joys and the lessons from challenges.

8. **Freedom from Attachment:** Inner peace involves letting go of excessive attachment to material possessions, outcomes, or the opinions of others. This freedom from attachment reduces stress and fosters contentment.

9. **Patience and Tolerance:** Patience and tolerance are hallmark traits of those who have achieved inner peace. They approach life's irritations and setbacks with grace and understanding.

Overall, inner peace is a state of holistic well-being that permeates all aspects of life, allowing individuals to experience greater joy, contentment, and fulfillment.

## Differences Between Inner Peace and External Calm

Inner peace and external calm both involve a sense of tranquility, but they differ significantly in their origins and resilience. Inner peace is an internal state of mental and emotional stability that arises from within. It is characterized by a deep sense of contentment and acceptance that remains unaffected by external circumstances. This enduring state allows individuals to navigate challenges gracefully and with composure, fostering emotional resilience and well-being. Inner peace is cultivated through mindfulness and meditation, providing a sustainable foundation for lasting happiness.

In contrast, external calm is a temporary state of tranquility that depends on the surrounding environment. It is often achieved through quiet or peaceful settings and can be easily disrupted by external changes such as noise or conflict. While external calm offers short-term relief and relaxation, it lacks the depth and stability of inner peace. External calm can be fleeting because it relies on external conditions and does not necessarily contribute to long-term well-being. Ultimately, while external calm can provide a momentary respite, inner peace offers a profound and enduring sense of balance that enriches every aspect of life.

## Importance of Inner Peace for Mental and Emotional Well-Being

Inner peace plays a crucial role in enhancing mental and emotional well-being. It provides a stable foundation that allows individuals to remain calm and centered despite life's challenges and uncertainties. By cultivating inner peace, people can experience a greater sense of clarity, focus, and emotional resilience, which helps them navigate stress and adversity gracefully. This inner tranquility reduces anxiety and prevents emotional turmoil, enabling individuals to maintain a balanced and positive outlook.

Moreover, inner peace fosters self-awareness and acceptance, allowing individuals to understand their thoughts and emotions without judgment. This self-awareness leads to healthier relationships, promoting empathy and compassion toward oneself and others. With inner peace, individuals can release negative emotions and attachments, creating space for joy, gratitude, and contentment. Ultimately, inner peace is essential for mental and emotional well-being, as it empowers individuals to live more fulfilling and harmonious lives, regardless of external circumstances.

## 3.2 INNER PEACE IN DAILY LIFE

Inner peace is essential to a balanced and fulfilling life, allowing individuals to navigate daily challenges gracefully and with composure. Incorporating inner peace into everyday life involves cultivating habits and practices that promote mental and emotional stability. Let us explore how to integrate inner peace into daily activities:

1. **Start with Mindful Mornings:** Begin your day with a few moments of mindfulness or meditation. This practice sets a calm and upbeat tone for the day, helping you to stay centered and focused. Incorporate a gratitude practice by reflecting on three things you are grateful for each morning. This shifts your mindset to one of appreciation and positivity.
2. **Practice Mindfulness Throughout the Day:** Engage in activities with full awareness and presence. Whether eating, walking, or working, focus on the task and avoid multitasking. Take short breaks during the day to practice mindful breathing or meditation. This can help reset your mind and reduce stress.
3. **Cultivate Emotional Awareness:** Pay attention to your emotions without judgment. Acknowledge your feelings and allow yourself to

process them rather than suppress them—practice self-compassion by treating yourself with kindness and understanding, especially during difficult times.

4. **Create a Peaceful Environment:** Organize your physical space to promote calm and relaxation. Declutter your surroundings and incorporate soothing elements like plants, soft lighting, and calming colors. Designate a quiet area in your home where you can retreat for meditation, reflection, or relaxation.

5. **Foster Positive Relationships:** Surround yourself with supportive and positive people who uplift and encourage you. Healthy relationships contribute significantly to inner peace. Practice active listening and empathy in your interactions with others. This strengthens your relationships and fosters a sense of connection and understanding.

# Examples of Inner Peace Practices in Various Places

**At Work:**

- Begin your workday with a brief meditation or deep breathing exercise to clear your mind and focus your intentions.

- Set realistic goals and prioritize tasks to manage your workload effectively. Break tasks into smaller steps and tackle them individually to avoid feeling overwhelmed.
- Incorporate short breaks to stretch, walk, or practice mindfulness, which can help maintain energy and reduce stress throughout the day.

**At Home:**

- Establish a daily routine that includes time for relaxation and self-care, such as reading, journaling, or taking a warm bath.
- Practice gratitude with your family by sharing appreciation and positive experiences during meals or gatherings.
- Engage in activities that bring joy and relaxation, such as gardening, cooking, or listening to music.

**In Social Interactions:**

- Approach conversations with an open mind and heart, listening attentively and without judgment.
- Practice forgiveness by letting go of grudges and resentment. This will free you from emotional burdens and promote inner peace.
- Set healthy boundaries in relationships to protect your well-being and ensure balanced interactions.

# Exercises and Reflections to Cultivate Inner Peace

1. **Daily Mindfulness Exercise**: Set aside 5-10 minutes daily for a mindfulness practice. Focus on your breath and observe your thoughts without judgment. Allow yourself to be present in the moment.
2. **Gratitude Journaling:** Write down three things you are grateful for at the end of each day. Reflect on these moments and how they contributed to your peace and well-being.
3. **Emotional Reflection:** Reflect on your emotions and experiences. Ask yourself, "What am I feeling right now?" and "What can I learn from this experience?" This practice enhances self-awareness and emotional resilience.
4. **Visualization Exercise:** Visualize a place or situation that brings peace and joy. Immerse yourself in the details, such as sights, sounds, and sensations, to create a calming mental retreat.
5. **Loving-Kindness Meditation**: Practice loving-kindness meditation by silently repeating phrases of goodwill toward yourself and others. For example, "May I be happy, healthy, and live with ease." Extend these wishes to loved ones and eventually to all beings.

Incorporating inner peace into daily life enhances mental and emotional well-being, transforming everyday activities through mindfulness, gratitude, and self-awareness. Inner peace is a continuous journey that enriches life and empowers individuals to navigate challenges with resilience and grace. It's not just the absence of stress but a profound sense of harmony within oneself. Here are several effective techniques to help cultivate inner peace:

**Meditation and Breathing Exercises**

- **Mindfulness Meditation**: It involves focusing on the present moment without judgment. It helps calm the mind, increase self-awareness, and reduce stress. Sit comfortably in a quiet place, close your eyes, and focus on your breath. Observe your thoughts and sensations without getting attached to them. Return your focus to your breath whenever your mind wanders.
- **Loving-Kindness Meditation:** Metta meditation involves sending goodwill and positive thoughts to yourself and others, promoting compassion and connection. Begin silently repeating phrases like "May I be happy, may I be healthy, may I be at peace." Gradually extend

these wishes to loved ones, acquaintances, and even those in conflict.

**Breathing Exercises:**

- **Deep Breathing:** Inhaling deeply through the nose, holding for a few seconds, and exhaling slowly through the mouth helps activate the parasympathetic nervous system, promoting relaxation and reducing stress.
- **Box Breathing:** This technique involves inhaling for four counts, holding the breath for four counts, exhaling for four counts, and pausing for four counts before repeating. It helps stabilize your mood and calm the mind.
- **Alternate Nostril Breathing:** In yoga, this technique balances the body's energy and reduces stress. Close your right nostril with your thumb and inhale deeply through the left nostril. Close the left nostril with your finger, release the right nostril, and exhale through the right. Repeat, alternating nostrils.

**Mindfulness Practices**

- **Mindful Walking:** Engage in walking meditation by paying attention to each step, the sensation of your feet touching the ground, and the rhythm of your breath. This practice helps you stay present and connected to your surroundings.

- **Mindful Eating:** Eat slowly and savor each bite, noticing the flavors, textures, and aromas of your food. This practice enhances your appreciation for your meals and promotes better digestion and mindfulness.
- **Body Scan:** Lie down comfortably and mentally scan your body from head to toe, observing any areas of tension or discomfort. This practice increases body awareness and helps release physical stress.

**Creating a Peaceful Environment**

- **Decluttering:** A tidy, organized space can reduce mental clutter and stress. Regularly clean and declutter your living and working spaces to create a calm and inviting atmosphere.
- **Incorporating Nature:** Surround yourself with natural elements like plants, flowers, or water features. Nature has a calming effect and can enhance your sense of well-being.
- **Soothing Colors and Lighting**: Use calming colors like blues, greens, and neutrals in your decor. Soft lighting, such as candles or dimmable lamps, can also create a relaxing ambiance.

## Managing Stress and Anxiety

- **Time Management:** Prioritize tasks and set realistic goals to manage your time effectively. Break tasks into smaller, manageable steps to avoid feeling overwhelmed.
- **Setting Boundaries:** Learn to say no to commitments that do not align with your values or well-being. Protect your time and energy by setting healthy boundaries with others.
- **Journaling:** Write about your thoughts, feelings, and experiences to process emotions and gain clarity. Journaling can help you identify stressors and develop strategies for coping with them.

## Positive Thinking and Gratitude

- **Affirmations:** Positive affirmations reinforce self-belief and cultivate a positive mindset. Repeat statements like "I am at peace" or "I choose happiness" to shift your focus to positivity.
- **Gratitude Practice:** Regularly reflect on the things you are grateful for. Keeping a gratitude journal can help you focus on the positive aspects of your life and foster contentment.

## Building Healthy Relationships

- **Active Listening:** Practice active listening by giving your full attention to others when they speak. This fosters deeper connections and understanding.
- **Empathy and Compassion:** Cultivate empathy and compassion towards others. Recognizing and appreciating different perspectives can enhance relationships and create a sense of belonging.
- **Letting Go of Grudges:** Release resentment and practice forgiveness to free yourself from negative emotions. Holding onto grudges can disrupt your peace and well-being.

**Engaging in Physical Activity**

- **Yoga and Tai Chi:** These practices combine movement, breath, and meditation to enhance physical and mental well-being. They promote flexibility, strength, and relaxation.
- **Regular Exercise:** Engage in regular physical activity, such as walking, running, or dancing, to release endorphins and reduce stress. Exercise is a powerful tool for enhancing mood and resilience.

Achieving inner peace requires a combination of mindfulness, intentional living, and self-awareness. Incorporating these techniques into daily life can cultivate a more profound sense of tranquility and resilience. Inner peace is not a destination but an ongoing journey that enriches your life and empowers you to face challenges with grace and clarity. Embrace these practices and allow them to guide you toward a more peaceful and fulfilling existence.

## Real-Life Examples and Case Studies of Successful Stress Management

- Jane, a marketing executive, managed her stress by incorporating regular exercise, practicing mindfulness, and setting realistic work goals. This helped her stay calm and focused, even during busy periods.
- Mark, a college student, used deep breathing exercises, maintained a gratitude journal, and sought support from friends and family to manage his anxiety. These practices improved his mental health and academic performance.
- Lisa, a mother of two, created a peaceful home environment, practiced yoga, and took regular breaks to meditate. These strategies helped her maintain inner peace while balancing work and family demands.

Finding inner peace is a continuous journey that requires practice and commitment. You can cultivate a sense of tranquility and resilience by understanding its nature and integrating practical techniques, such as meditation, creating a peaceful environment, and managing stress. Inner peace is the foundation for overall well-being, allowing you to navigate life's challenges gracefully and calmly. The next chapter will explore defining your purpose and how it contributes to a joyful and fulfilling life.

# 4 Defining Your Purpose

"The purpose of life is not to be happy. It is to be useful, to be honorable, to be compassionate, to have it make some difference that you have lived and lived well." – Ralph Waldo Emerson.

Defining your purpose is a critical step in achieving lasting joy and fulfillment. A clear sense of purpose gives our lives direction, motivation, and meaning. It helps us navigate challenges, make decisions, and focus on what truly matters. In this chapter, we will explore the importance of having a purpose, share inspiring stories of purpose-driven lives, and provide practical exercises to help you discover and align with your purpose.

## 4.1 Importance of Purpose

Having a sense of purpose significantly enhances happiness and well-being, as supported by both research and personal stories. A study by the University of Michigan found that individuals with a strong sense of purpose report higher life satisfaction and overall well-being. These individuals are likelier to experience positive emotions, maintain better physical health, and enjoy longer lives. Purpose provides direction, motivation, and resilience, helping people persevere through challenges and leading to a more fulfilling life.

One compelling example is the story of Emma, who discovered her calling in advocating for environmental conservation. Her deep passion for preserving the environment brought her immense joy and satisfaction. Emma found personal fulfillment by dedicating her time and efforts to this cause and inspired others to join her. Her commitment led to the creation of a community of like-minded individuals striving toward the common goal of environmental preservation. Emma's work catalyzed change, demonstrating how a strong sense of purpose can create a ripple effect, spreading positivity and inspiring collective action.

Similarly, John's story highlights the transformative impact of purpose. As a teacher and mentor, John found his purpose in educating and inspiring young students. His dedication to fostering a love for learning and personal growth not only enriched his own life but also profoundly impacted the lives of his students. John's commitment to education helped create an environment where students could thrive, learn, and develop into well-rounded individuals. His influence extended far beyond the classroom, as his students carried the lessons and values they learned into their futures, spreading the benefits of his purposeful work. John's story illustrates how living with purpose can create lasting, positive change in others' lives.

These stories show how a clear sense of purpose can profoundly impact personal happiness and well-being. Purpose-driven individuals find deep joy and fulfillment in their pursuits, and their actions inspire and uplift others, creating a positive ripple effect that extends far beyond themselves.

**Exercises to Explore Personal Purpose and Meaning:** To explore and clarify your purpose, consider engaging in the following exercises:

- **Reflect on Fulfillment and Satisfaction:** Write about times when you felt most fulfilled and satisfied. What activities were you engaged in, and what values were you honoring during these moments? Identifying the elements contributing to your fulfillment can provide insights into your true passions and purpose.
- **Create a Vision Board:** Use images, words, and symbols to create a vision board that represents your dreams, goals, and the impact you want to have on the world. This visual representation can help you clarify your aspirations and stay focused on your purpose, constantly reminding you of what you are working towards.

- **Reflect on Your Legacy:** Consider how you want to be remembered and what legacy you wish to leave behind. Reflecting on your desired impact can help you align your actions with your long-term goals and values, ensuring that you live a life of purpose and significance.

These exercises can help you uncover your purpose and meaning, providing direction and motivation to live a more purposeful and fulfilling life. By understanding what truly matters to you, you can make conscious choices that align with your values and contribute to your happiness and well-being.

**Purpose-Driven Life Stories:** Purpose-driven individuals often find profound joy and fulfillment by dedicating themselves to meaningful causes, leaving a lasting impact on the world. Here are some inspiring examples:

- **Malala Yousafzai:** Malala found her purpose in advocating for girls' education worldwide. Despite life-threatening adversity, her unwavering commitment to education brought her immense joy and sparked significant global change, making her a symbol of courage and resilience.
- **Steve Jobs:** The co-founder of Apple Inc., Steve Jobs, lived with a clear purpose to innovate and

revolutionize technology. His passion for blending technology with artistry led to groundbreaking products like the iPhone and MacBook, leaving a lasting legacy in multiple industries.

- **Mother Teresa:** Known for her selfless service to the poor, she dedicated her life to helping those in need. Her work through the Missionaries of Charity exemplifies the impact of a purpose-driven life, inspiring generations to engage in acts of kindness and humanitarian work.

These stories highlight the power of purpose in driving resilience, personal growth, and fulfillment. Purpose fuels perseverance through challenges, evolves with experiences, and aligns actions with one's deepest values. You can cultivate a life of meaning and joy by staying open to discovering your purpose, embracing challenges as opportunities, and aligning your actions with your purpose.

**Practical Takeaways:**

- **Stay Open to Discovering Your Purpose:** Explore different paths and experiences to uncover what truly matters to you, understanding that purpose can evolve.
- **Embrace Challenges as Opportunities:** View difficulties as catalysts for growth and resilience,

using them to strengthen your commitment to your goals.

- **Align Actions with Purpose:** Regularly reflect on your actions to ensure they align with your core values, leading to a more coherent and fulfilling life.

These insights guide living purposefully, leading to a more profound sense of meaning and satisfaction. Satisfaction.

## 4.2 Discovering Your Purpose

Discovering your purpose is a transformative journey that involves self-reflection, understanding your passions and strengths, and setting meaningful goals. It requires introspection and exploration to uncover what truly drives you and aligns with your values and aspirations. This section will explore practical exercises and tools to help you discover your purpose, identify your passions and strengths, and set goals that lead to a fulfilling and purposeful life. Self-reflection is a powerful tool for uncovering your purpose. It involves asking yourself meaningful questions and engaging in practices that encourage introspection and insight. Questions and Prompts to Help Uncover Personal Purpose:

## What activities make you lose track of time because you enjoy them so much?

Reflect on the activities that absorb you so completely that time seems to fly by. You are often passionate about these things and can explain your purpose. Consider how you feel when engaged in these activities and what aspects bring you joy and fulfillment.

## What are the most critical values in your life?

Identifying your core values is essential to discovering your purpose. Reflect on the principles and beliefs that guide your actions and decisions. Consider how these values influence your life choices and how you can align them with your purpose.

## What problems or issues are you passionate about solving?

Think about the challenges and issues that ignite your passion and concern. These are often areas where you feel compelled to make a difference. Consider how you can contribute to solving these problems and your role in creating positive change.

## Techniques for Deep Reflection and Introspection

- **Journaling:** Journaling is a powerful tool for self-reflection. Regularly writing about your thoughts, feelings, and experiences can help you uncover patterns and insights. Reflect on your entries to identify recurring themes and ideas that resonate with you.
- **Meditation:** Meditation provides a quiet space for reflection and introspection. Spend silence, focusing on your breath and allowing your thoughts to flow naturally. Use this time to reflect on your life, goals, and aspirations and clarify your purpose.
- **Discussions:** Engage in conversations with trusted friends or mentors who know you well. Discuss your passions, strengths, and goals with them to gain new perspectives and insights. Others may see qualities and potential in you that you might overlook.

**Examples of Reflective Practices**

- **Spend Time in Nature**: Spend time in nature to disconnect from daily distractions. Whether hiking in the mountains, walking in a park, or sitting by a lake, nature provides a peaceful environment for connecting with your inner self and reflecting on your purpose.

- **Engage in Creative Activities:** Creativity can be a powerful way to express your thoughts and feelings. Engage in activities like drawing, painting, writing, or playing music to tap into your subconscious and explore your purpose through creative expression.
- **Volunteer for Causes You Care About:** Volunteering allows you to engage with causes that resonate with your values and interests. It provides opportunities to see how different issues affect communities and how you can contribute to positive change. Volunteering can reveal new aspects of your purpose and passions.

**Identifying Passions and Strengths:** Identifying your passions and strengths is crucial in discovering your purpose. It involves exploring what excites you and understanding your skills and talents. Methods to Discover What You Are Passionate About

- **Try New Activities and Hobbies:** Experiment with different activities and hobbies to explore what excites and energizes you. This exploration can help you identify new interests and passions that align with your purpose.
- **Reflect on Past Experiences:** Reflect on experiences where you felt profoundly engaged

and satisfied. Consider what aspects of these experiences contributed to your fulfillment and how they align with your interests and values.
- **Seek Feedback from Others:** Ask friends, family, or colleagues for feedback on what they perceive as your passions and strengths. Others may offer insights you may not have considered and highlight areas where you naturally excel.

## Assessing Personal Strengths and How to Leverage Them

- **Take Personality and Strength Assessments:** Utilize tools like the VIA Character Strengths survey or StrengthsFinder to identify your natural talents and strengths. These assessments provide insights into your unique abilities and how to leverage them to pursue your purpose.
- **Reflect on Compliments and Positive Feedback:** Pay attention to compliments and positive feedback you receive from others. These insights can reveal areas where you excel and guide you in identifying your strengths and how they can contribute to your purpose.
- **Consider How Your Strengths Can Be Applied**: Reflect on how your strengths can be

applied to your passions and purpose. Consider how your unique talents can contribute to positive change and how you can use them to make a meaningful impact. This realization can inspire and motivate you to take action.

**Exercises and Tools for Self-Assessment**

- **SWOT Analysis:** Conduct a SWOT analysis to identify your strengths, weaknesses, opportunities, and threats. This tool provides a comprehensive understanding of yourself and helps you identify areas for growth and improvement.
- **Ikigai Diagram:** The Ikigai diagram helps you find the intersection of what you love, what you are good at, what the world needs, and what you can be paid for. This tool provides a holistic approach to discovering your purpose and aligning it with your career and life goals.
- **Reflective Journals:** Keep a reflective journal to document your thoughts, experiences, and insights as you explore your passions and strengths. Regular reflection can be enlightening, helping you identify patterns, clarify your purpose, and increase your self-awareness.

**Setting Meaningful Goals:** Setting meaningful goals is essential for aligning your actions with your purpose. It involves defining clear objectives and creating a plan to achieve them. Following are steps to Set and Achieve Goals Aligned with Your Purpose.

- **Define Clear, Specific, and Measurable Goals:** Set clear, specific, and measurable goals. Ensure that they align with your purpose and reflect your values and aspirations. Clear goals provide direction and motivation.
- **Break Down Larger Goals into Smaller Steps:** Divide larger goals into smaller, manageable steps. Breaking goals down makes them more achievable and helps you maintain focus and momentum.
- **Create an Action Plan with Deadlines and Milestones**: Develop an action plan with deadlines and milestones to track your progress. Review your plan regularly to ensure you are on track and adjust as needed.

### Techniques for Maintaining Motivation and Focus

- **Visualize Your Goals:** Regularly visualize your goals and their positive impact on your life and

others. Visualization reinforces your commitment to your purpose and helps you stay motivated.
- **Celebrate Small Achievements:** Celebrate small achievements and milestones along the way. Recognizing progress boosts motivation and builds momentum toward larger goals.
- **Surround Yourself with Supportive People:** Surround yourself with supportive people who encourage and inspire you. A strong support network provides motivation and accountability as you pursue your purpose.

**Real-Life Examples and Success Stories**

- **Sarah's Nonprofit Organization:** Sarah set a goal to start a nonprofit organization focused on literacy. She achieved her dream by breaking it into actionable steps, seeking mentorship, and staying committed to her purpose. Her organization has positively impacted countless individuals, enhancing their literacy skills and opportunities.
- **Tom's Musical Journey:** Tom, a musician passionate about bringing joy through music, set goals to perform in local venues, record an album, and teach music to underprivileged children. His dedication to his purpose brought fulfillment and

success, creating positivity and inspiration in his community.

- **Lisa's Mental Health Advocacy:** Lisa wanted to improve mental health awareness and set goals to write a blog, organize community events, and collaborate with mental health professionals. Her efforts significantly impacted raising awareness and providing resources to those in need. Lisa's purpose-driven journey brought her immense satisfaction and contributed to positive change.

Discovering your purpose is a transformative self-reflection, exploration, and goal-setting journey. By identifying your passions and strengths and setting meaningful goals, you can align your actions with your purpose, leading to a life of joy, fulfillment, and impact. Embrace this journey as it guides you toward a life of meaning and significance. The next chapter will explore personal growth, another essential element in pursuing daily joy.

# 5 Embracing Personal Growth

"Personal growth is not a matter of learning new information but unlearning old limits." – Alan Cohen.

Embracing personal growth is essential for achieving lasting joy and fulfillment. It involves a commitment to continuous learning, self-improvement, and overcoming challenges. Personal growth enhances our abilities and knowledge and fosters resilience, adaptability, and a more profound sense of purpose. This chapter will explore the principles of a growth mindset, the benefits of personal development, and practical strategies to foster personal growth.

## 5.1 The Journey of Growth

Personal growth is a transformative process that enhances various aspects of our lives, leading to greater happiness and success. This journey involves adopting a growth mindset, focusing on personal development, and leveraging the benefits of continuous improvement. Let's explore the critical elements of this journey and the impact it can have on your life.

**Growth Mindset vs. Fixed Mindset**

A growth mindset is the belief that abilities and intelligence can be developed through dedication, effort, and hard work. This concept, popularized by psychologist Carol Dweck, emphasizes the importance of learning and improvement over relying solely on innate talent. People with a growth mindset see challenges as opportunities to grow and view failures as valuable learning experiences. A love of learning drives them, and they are willing to put in the effort needed to develop their skills and abilities.

In contrast, a fixed mindset is the belief that abilities are static and unchangeable. Individuals with a fixed mindset tend to avoid challenges, fearing failure will reveal their limitations. They often give up easily when faced with obstacles because they believe their abilities are predetermined and cannot be improved. This mindset limits personal growth and development, discouraging risk-taking and trying new things.

**Benefits of Adopting a Growth Mindset**

- **Increased Motivation and Resilience:** A growth mindset leads to higher motivation and resilience. People who believe they can improve their abilities are more likely to take on challenges and persist despite setbacks. This resilience fosters a strong sense of determination and perseverance.
- **Enhanced Creativity and Innovation:** With a growth mindset, individuals are more open to

experimentation and exploration. They are less afraid of failure and more willing to try new ideas, which fosters creativity and innovation.
- **Improved Relationships:** A growth mindset also benefits relationships. People who embrace this mindset are more open to feedback and view criticism as opportunities for improvement. They are more empathetic and willing to learn from others, which strengthens interpersonal connections.

## Examples of Growth Mindset in Action

- **Thomas Edison:** The light bulb inventor famously failed thousands of times before achieving success. Edison exemplified a growth mindset by viewing each failure as a step toward success, demonstrating persistence and resilience.
- **Serena Williams:** The world-renowned tennis player consistently seeks to improve her skills through rigorous training and learning from her matches. Her commitment to growth and relentless pursuit of excellence are testaments to her growth mindset.
- **J.K. Rowling:** The author of the Harry Potter series faced numerous rejections before her books were published. Rowling's perseverance in her

writing journey reflects the resilience and determination of a growth mindset, ultimately leading to her success.

## How Personal Growth Contributes to Overall Happiness and Success

- **Enhanced Self-Awareness:** Personal growth enhances self-awareness, helping individuals understand their strengths, weaknesses, and values. This self-knowledge leads to better decision-making and a greater sense of purpose, contributing to overall happiness.
- **Increased Confidence and Self-Esteem:** As individuals achieve new skills and overcome challenges, they experience a boost in confidence and self-esteem. This newfound confidence translates into more tremendous success in various aspects of life.
- **Fosters Resilience and Adaptability:** Personal development fosters resilience and adaptability, enabling individuals to easily navigate life's changes and challenges. This adaptability is crucial for maintaining well-being in an ever-changing world.

## Areas of Personal Development to Focus On

1. **Emotional Intelligence:** Developing self-awareness, empathy, and practical communication skills is vital for building strong relationships and navigating social interactions.
2. **Professional Skills:** Enhancing competencies relevant to one's career, such as leadership, technical skills, and project management, can lead to career advancement and fulfillment.
3. **Physical Health:** Prioritizing physical fitness, nutrition, and overall well-being is essential for maintaining energy and vitality.
4. **Mental Health:** Engaging in practices that promote mental clarity, stress management, and emotional balance is crucial for achieving a balanced and fulfilling life.

## Stories of Transformative Personal Growth

- **Alex's Career Transformation:** Alex transformed his career by continuously learning new technologies and earning certifications. His dedication to personal growth eventually led him to land his dream job as a lead software engineer, demonstrating the power of lifelong learning.
- **Maria's Leadership Journey:** Maria focused on developing her emotional intelligence, which improved her relationships and made her a more

effective leader in her organization. Her commitment to personal growth allowed her to excel professionally and personally.

- **John's Health Transformation:** John dedicated time to improving his physical health through regular exercise and a balanced diet. His commitment to personal growth increased energy, confidence, and overall well-being, illustrating the profound impact of prioritizing health.

The growth journey involves embracing a growth mindset, focusing on personal development, and pursuing continuous improvement. A growth mindset boosts motivation, resilience, and creativity, leading to greater happiness and success. Individuals thrive in various life aspects by enhancing self-awareness, confidence, and adaptability, enriching their fulfillment and success.

## 5.2 STRATEGIES FOR PERSONAL GROWTH

Personal growth is a lifelong journey of continuous learning, seeking feedback, and overcoming challenges. By adopting effective strategies, individuals can enhance their skills, build resilience, and achieve greater fulfillment. Continuous learning keeps the mind sharp, fosters adaptability, and opens new opportunities, helping individuals stay relevant and reach their full personal and professional potential.

## Techniques for Acquiring New Skills

- **Set Specific, Achievable Goals:** Define clear objectives for what you want to learn and break the learning process into manageable steps. This approach makes it easier to track progress and maintain motivation.
- **Utilize a Variety of Learning Resources:** Explore different learning platforms and resources, such as online courses, books, workshops, and mentorship programs. Engaging with diverse learning methods can provide a well-rounded understanding of the subject.
- **Practice Regularly:** Apply new skills in real-life situations to reinforce learning and build confidence. Consistent practice helps solidify knowledge and improves proficiency over time.

## Examples of Skills That Enhance Personal Growth

- **Learning a New Language:** Acquiring a new language improves cognitive abilities and enhances cultural awareness, providing personal and professional opportunities.

- **Developing Public Speaking Skills:** Effective communication is valuable in any field. Improving public speaking skills boosts confidence and enhances interpersonal interactions.
- **Acquiring Technical Skills:** Learning coding, graphic design, or data analysis can expand career prospects and unleash creativity, enabling individuals to innovate and solve complex problems.

**How to Seek and Use Feedback Effectively**

- **Approach Feedback with an Open Mind:** View feedback as an opportunity for growth rather than criticism. Be receptive to suggestions and consider how they can help you improve.
- **Ask Specific Questions:** Gain clarity and actionable insights by asking focused questions like "What areas do you think I could improve in?" This encourages constructive feedback that can guide your development.
- **Reflect and Act:** Reflect on the feedback received and create an action plan to address areas of improvement. Implementing feedback demonstrates a commitment to growth and a proactive attitude.

**Benefits of Constructive Criticism**

- **Identifying Blind Spots:** Constructive criticism provides valuable insights into areas needing improvement, helping you identify blind spots and make informed changes.
- **Fostering Continuous Improvement:** Constructive feedback encourages a culture of continuous improvement and mutual support in both personal and professional settings.
- **Enhancing Credibility and Trust:** Embracing and using feedback to improve builds credibility and trust with others, showcasing your dedication to personal and professional growth.

## Exercises to Practice Receiving and Acting on Feedback

- **Role-Play Scenarios:** Practice receiving and responding to feedback by role-playing scenarios with a trusted friend or colleague. This exercise helps you develop practical communication skills and confidence in handling feedback.
- **Feedback Journal:** Keep a journal to document the feedback received, your reflections, and the action steps you take to address it. This practice provides a record of your progress and helps you stay accountable.

- **Seek Diverse Perspectives:** Regularly seek feedback from various sources, such as peers, mentors, and supervisors, to gain a well-rounded understanding of your strengths and areas for improvement.

## Strategies to Manage and Overcome Fear

- **Reframe Failure as a Learning Opportunity:** Shift your perspective by viewing failure as a valuable learning experience rather than a setback. Focus on what you can learn from each experience and how it can contribute to your growth.
- **Embrace a Growth Mindset:** Cultivate a growth mindset by embracing challenges and viewing effort as a path to mastery. This mindset encourages resilience and perseverance in the face of adversity.
- **Practice Self-Compassion:** Treat yourself with kindness and understanding when encountering setbacks. Remember that failure is a natural part of the growth process and an opportunity for growth.

## How to View Failure as a Learning Opportunity

- **Analyze What Went Wrong:** Reflect on the factors that contributed to the failure and identify areas for improvement. Use this analysis to inform future actions and decisions.
- **Celebrate Effort and Progress:** Acknowledge your effort and progress, even if the outcome wasn't as expected. Recognize that each step forward is valuable and contributes to your journey.
- **Share Experiences and Seek Support:** Discuss your experiences with others and seek advice and encouragement. Learning from others' perspectives can provide new insights and help you feel supported in your growth journey.

**Inspirational Stories of Overcoming Failure**

- **Oprah Winfrey:** Oprah faced numerous personal and professional setbacks, including being fired from her first television job. She used these experiences to fuel her determination and became a media mogul and philanthropist, exemplifying resilience and perseverance.
- **Michael Jordan:** After being cut from his high school basketball team, Michael Jordan used this perceived failure as motivation to work harder. His dedication and relentless pursuit of excellence

made him one of the greatest basketball players ever.

- **J.K. Rowling:** Before achieving success with the Harry Potter series, J.K. Rowling faced multiple rejections from publishers. Her persistence and belief in her work exemplify the power of resilience and the importance of perseverance in the face of failure.

Personal growth is a lifelong journey of learning new skills, seeking feedback, and overcoming challenges. By adopting a growth mindset and embracing continuous learning, individuals can unlock their potential, achieve greater fulfillment, and enhance their happiness and success. This journey fosters resilience, adaptability, and a more profound sense of purpose. As you continue this path, you'll be better equipped to integrate joy into your daily life, creating a foundation for lasting happiness and fulfillment.

# 6 INTEGRATING JOY INTO DAILY LIFE

"Find out where joy resides, and give it a voice far beyond singing. For to miss the joy is to miss all." – Robert Louis Stevenson.

Integrating joy into daily life is about consistently cultivating habits and practices that allow you to experience and sustain joy. It involves making intentional choices that prioritize your well-being and happiness. This chapter will explore daily joy practices, including morning routines, finding joy in small moments, and building joyful habits. We will also discuss maintaining joy during challenging times through resilience, positive thinking, and support systems.

## 6.1 DAILY JOY PRACTICES

Starting your day with joy sets a positive tone and influences your mood and productivity. A joyful morning routine can help you feel energized, focused, and ready to face any challenges that come your way.

**Importance of a Joyful Start to the Day:** Establishing a joyful morning routine creates a foundation for a joyous day. Starting your day with activities that uplift and energize you impacts your overall mood, increases productivity, and enhances your ability to handle stress. Setting aside time each morning for practices that bring joy and fulfillment creates a mindset prioritizing well-being and happiness throughout the day. Let me share with you some examples of Morning Routines That Enhance Joy.

- **Begin with Gratitude:** Take a few minutes to reflect on what you are grateful for. This practice can shift your mindset to appreciation and positivity, setting a joyful tone for the day.
- **Engage in Physical Activity:** Whether a short walk, yoga, or a workout, physical activity releases endorphins, the body's natural mood enhancers, and boosts energy levels.
- **Mindful Breakfast:** Prepare and enjoy a nutritious breakfast mindfully, savoring each bite and appreciating the nourishment it provides.

**Tips for Creating Your Morning Routine**

- **Personalize Your Routine:** Choose activities that inspire and bring you joy. This could be reading, journaling, meditating, or listening to uplifting music.
- **Start Small:** Begin with a few activities and gradually build your routine as you become more comfortable. Small, consistent efforts can lead to significant positive changes over time.

- **Consistency is Key:** Try to stick to your routine regularly to establish it as a habit. Consistency helps reinforce the positive impact of your morning practices.

**Joy in Small Moments:** Joy can be found in simple, everyday moments if we pay attention. Embracing these moments with mindfulness and gratitude can significantly enhance our overall sense of happiness. Joy is often hidden in the small, ordinary moments of life. By approaching activities like drinking a cup of tea, watching a sunset, or chatting with a friend with mindfulness and gratitude, you can transform them into sources of joy. Paying attention to these moments helps cultivate a deeper appreciation for life's simple pleasures. Find some Mindfulness Techniques to Enhance our Daily Joy.

- **Practice Mindful Breathing:** Take deep breaths and focus on the present moment. This practice helps you stay grounded and appreciate the beauty around you.
- **Engage Your Senses:** Notice the sights, sounds, smells, tastes, and textures in your environment. This heightened awareness can turn ordinary moments into joyful experiences.

- **Slow down:** Avoid rushing through tasks. Take your time to engage in and enjoy what you are doing entirely.

**Real-Life Examples and Exercises**

- **Turn Chores into Joy:** Listen to your favorite music or podcast while washing dishes or doing laundry. This can make mundane tasks more enjoyable.
- **Practice a Daily Gratitude Ritual:** At the end of each day, write down three things that brought you joy. Reflecting on these moments can enhance your overall sense of happiness.
- **Joyful Pauses:** Set reminders on your phone to take short breaks throughout the day to stretch, breathe, or appreciate the moment.

**Building Joyful Habits:** Developing and maintaining habits that bring joy is crucial for integrating joy into daily life. These habits help create a foundation for lasting happiness and well-being. Following are some steps to Develop and Maintain Habits That Bring Joy.

- **Identify Activities That Bring You Joy:** Make a conscious effort to incorporate activities that bring joy into your routine. Prioritize these activities to ensure they become regular parts of your day.

- **Start with Small, Manageable Actions:** Begin with small steps and gradually build them into habits. For example, if you enjoy reading, start with a few pages daily and gradually increase the time.
- **Track Your Progress and Celebrate Small Wins:** Keep track of your progress and celebrate small achievements to stay motivated and encouraged.

## Examples of Joyful Habits

- **Morning Walks or Runs in Nature:** Regular exercise in nature can boost mood and energy levels.
- **Daily Meditation or Mindfulness Practice:** Mindfulness practices can enhance mental clarity and emotional well-being.
- **Regular Creative Activities:** Participating in creative activities, such as painting, writing, or playing an instrument, can provide joy and fulfillment.
- **Volunteering or Helping Others:** Engaging in acts of kindness and service can bring joy and a sense of purpose.

## Techniques for Habit Formation and Maintenance

- **Use Habit Stacking:** Pair a new habit with an existing one. For example, meditate right after brushing your teeth in the morning to establish a routine.
- **Set Reminders:** Use alarms or notes to remind yourself to engage in joyful habits. This helps reinforce consistency.
- **Be Patient and Persistent:** Building new habits takes time. Stay committed, and don't get discouraged by setbacks. Persistence is key to habit formation.

### 6.2 Maintaining Joy Through Challenges

Maintaining joy during challenging times requires resilience, positive thinking, and finding joy in small things. The following strategies can help you navigate difficulties gracefully and maintain a positive outlook.

- **Focus on What You Can Control:** Identify aspects of the situation you can influence and take positive actions. This helps reduce feelings of helplessness.
- **Practice Self-Care:** Prioritize your physical and mental health through rest, nutrition, and

activities that recharge you. Self-care is essential for maintaining resilience.

- **Seek Joy in Small Things:** Small moments can provide comfort and relief even during difficult times. Look for simple pleasures and moments of gratitude.

## Techniques for Resilience and Positive Thinking

- **Reframe Negative Thoughts:** Challenge and reframe negative thoughts to find a more positive perspective. This helps maintain a balanced mindset.
- **Practice Acceptance:** Acknowledge and accept your emotions without judgment. Acceptance allows you to process and move through complicated feelings.
- **Visualize Positive Outcomes:** Imagine successful and joyful outcomes to reinforce a positive mindset and increase motivation.

## Examples of Overcoming Adversity with Joy

- **Jane's Story:** Jane found joy in gardening during a challenging period of unemployment, which provided her with a sense of purpose and tranquility.

- **Tom's Story:** Tom used humor and laughter to cope with a severe illness, improving his mood and strengthening his resolve to fight the disease.
- **Lisa's Story:** Lisa practiced gratitude and focused on the support she received from friends and family during a difficult divorce, helping her maintain a positive outlook.

**Resilience and Positive Thinking:** Resilience and positive thinking are essential for sustaining long-term joy and well-being. These qualities help you bounce back from setbacks and maintain a positive outlook despite challenges. Resilience is the ability to recover from setbacks and adapt to adversity. It is crucial for sustaining long-term joy and a positive outlook even in difficult times. Building resilience involves developing skills to manage stress, regulate emotions, and remain optimistic in facing challenges.

**Techniques to Develop a Positive Mindset**

- **Cultivate Optimism:** Focus on the positives and look for silver linings under challenging situations. This mindset shift can enhance resilience and well-being.
- **Practice Gratitude Regularly:** Regularly express gratitude for the positive aspects of your

life. This practice shifts your focus from what's lacking to what's abundant.
- **Engage in Positive Self-Talk:** Encourage and affirm yourself with positive and constructive thoughts. Positive self-talk boosts confidence and motivation.

**Stories and Exercises for Building Resilience**

- **John's Story:** John used positive affirmations and goal-setting to rebuild his life after a significant career setback, finding renewed joy and success.
- **Maria's Story:** Maria practiced mindfulness and yoga to cope with the stress of a demanding job, building resilience and maintaining her well-being.
- **Exercises:** Write down past challenges you've overcome and the strengths you developed from those experiences. Reflect on how these strengths can help you face current and future challenges.

**Support Systems and Community:** Supportive relationships and communities are crucial in maintaining joy and resilience. Building and sustaining a support network can enhance your well-being and encourage you during challenging times. Firm, supportive relationships provide emotional support, encouragement, and a sense of belonging. They are crucial for maintaining joy and resilience, as they offer a network of people who can provide guidance, empathy, and companionship. We can build and sustain a supportive community in the following ways:

- **Foster Meaningful Connections:** Spend quality time with family and friends to build solid and supportive relationships.
- **Join Groups or Communities:** Participate in groups or communities with shared interests and values to create a sense of belonging and connection.
- **Offer Support to Others:** Supporting others can also enhance one's sense of joy and fulfillment. Acts of kindness and service strengthen community bonds.

### Examples of Community Support in Action

- **Emma's Story:** Emma found joy and strength through her local running group, which provided camaraderie and motivation during tough times.
- **Alex's Story:** Alex joined a book club and discovered a supportive network of friends who shared his passion for reading and discussion.

- **Community Projects:** Participate in local volunteer efforts, which can create a sense of connection and purpose.

Integrating joy into daily life involves cultivating habits and practices prioritizing well-being and happiness. By establishing joyful morning routines, finding joy in small moments, and building joyful habits, you can create a foundation for lasting happiness. During challenging times, maintaining joy requires resilience, positive thinking, and the support of a strong community. These strategies will help you gracefully navigate life's ups and downs and maintain a joyful and fulfilling life. In the next chapter, we will explore case studies and personal stories to illustrate the transformative power of joy and how to apply these lessons to your own life.

# 7 CASE STUDIES AND PERSONAL STORIES

"Success is not the key to happiness. Happiness is the key to success. If you love what you are doing, you will be successful." – Albert Schweitzer.

Real-life examples and personal stories offer valuable insights into the practical application of finding joy in daily life. Learning from others' experiences can inspire us, identify effective strategies, and understand how to overcome challenges. In this chapter, we will explore personal anecdotes of individuals who have found joy, extract critical lessons from their journeys, and provide practical steps and reflective exercises to help you incorporate these teachings into your life.

## 7.1 REAL-LIFE EXAMPLES

**Sophia's Journey to Joy through Creativity:** Sophia, a marketing executive, felt overwhelmed by the demands of her job and struggled to find balance in her life. Rediscovering her love for painting, she began dedicating time to it every weekend. This creative outlet brought her immense joy and helped her balance her career's stress. Painting allowed her to express herself and tap into a part of her identity that was neglected due to work pressures.

Sophia's story highlights the importance of creative expression and balancing work with personal passions. Making time for hobbies can provide a sense of fulfillment and enhance well-being.

Initially, Sophia struggled with time management and felt guilty for taking time away from work. However, she found joy by setting aside specific times for her creative pursuits, ultimately improving her overall well-being.

**David's Transformation through Mindfulness:** David, a high school teacher, experienced burnout and dissatisfaction with his job. Seeking a change, he began practicing mindfulness and meditation daily. These practices helped him stay present, reduce stress, and rediscover joy in teaching. By incorporating mindfulness into his routine, David could manage classroom stress better and engage more meaningfully with his students.

David's journey underscores the power of mindfulness in enhancing mental health and the importance of daily practices for maintaining well-being. Self-care can significantly impact job satisfaction and personal happiness.

David first found it difficult to maintain a routine and questioned its effectiveness. Gradually, as he integrated mindfulness into his daily life, he noticed significant positive changes, reinforcing the value of consistency.

**Emily's Joyful Connection through Volunteering:** Emily, a retiree, felt isolated and unfulfilled after leaving her long-term career. To find a purpose, she began volunteering at a local animal shelter. This experience brought her deep joy and fulfillment, as she connected with the animals and other volunteers, enriching her life and providing a renewed sense of community.

Emily's story illustrates the value of community service and finding purpose in helping others. Building connections through volunteering can be a powerful source of joy and fulfillment.

Initially reluctant to step out of her comfort zone, Emily faced the challenge of finding a new role. However, she found joy and a new community by engaging in meaningful activities aligned with her values.

**Summary of Key Takeaways from Case Studies**

- Creative expression, mindfulness, and community service are potent sources of joy.
- Overcoming challenges often involves persistence, adaptability, and a willingness to explore new activities.
- Joy can be found in small, consistent practices that align with personal values and passions.

**Practical Applications for Readers**

- **Identify Joyful Activities:** Reflect on activities that bring you joy and dedicate regular time to them. Whether it's a hobby, exercise, or social activity, ensure it becomes a part of your routine.
- **Incorporate Mindfulness:** Practice mindfulness and self-care to enhance mental and emotional well-being. Simple meditation or mindful breathing practices can help reduce stress and increase happiness.
- **Engage in Community Service:** Find opportunities to volunteer or participate in community activities. This benefits others and enriches your life with a sense of purpose and connection.

**Reflective Questions to Apply Lessons to Your Life**

- What activities or hobbies bring you the most joy, and how can you incorporate them into your daily life?
- How can mindfulness practices help you stay present and reduce stress?
- What opportunities are there for you to engage in community service or volunteer work?

## 7.2 REFLECTION AND APPLICATION

Practical Steps to Incorporate Lessons into Daily Routines

- **Set Specific Goals:** Define clear goals for integrating joyful activities into your schedule. For example, dedicate 30 minutes each day to a hobby you enjoy or a mindfulness practice that centers you.
- **Create a Mindfulness Routine:** Establish daily mindfulness practices, such as morning meditation or mindful breathing exercises, to start your day with calm and presence.
- **Volunteer Regularly:** Seek out local organizations or causes that resonate with you and commit to volunteering. Engaging in community service can provide a sense of purpose and fulfillment.

**Exercises to Personalize and Apply the Teachings**

- **Joy Journal:** Keep a journal where you document moments of joy each day. Reflect on what brought you joy and how to create more moments.
- **Mindfulness Practice:** Choose a daily activity, such as eating or walking, and practice it

mindfully. Focus on your senses and stay fully present in the moment.
- **Community Engagement:** Identify a cause you care about and take the first step to get involved. Whether signing up for a volunteer event or reaching out to an organization, take action toward making a positive impact.

## Stories of Successful Application of These Lessons

- **Sophia's Continued Creative Growth:** After dedicating weekends to painting, Sophia expanded her creative pursuits by joining an art class. This enhanced her skills and connected her with a community of like-minded individuals, further enriching her life.
- **David's Mindful Classroom:** David introduced mindfulness practices to his students, creating a calmer and more focused classroom environment. His students benefited from the practices, and David found renewed joy in teaching.
- **Emily's Expanding Volunteer Efforts:** Emily's volunteering at the animal shelter led her to start a community garden project, combining her love for animals and nature. This new

endeavor brought her joy and connected her with more community members.

## Prompts and Activities for Deep Reflection

- Reflect on a recent moment of joy. What were you doing, and how did it make you feel? How can you create more of these moments in your daily life?
- Consider a challenge you've faced recently. How did you overcome it, and what did you learn from the experience? How can you apply these lessons to future challenges?
- Think about a time when you felt a strong sense of purpose. What were you involved in, and how did it impact your sense of joy and fulfillment?

## Journaling Exercises to Enhance Understanding

- **Daily Gratitude:** Write down three things you are grateful for and why each day. Reflect on how gratitude enhances your sense of joy.
- **Joy Mapping:** Create a visual map of activities, people, and places that bring you joy. Use this map to identify patterns and opportunities to incorporate joy into your life.
- **Resilience Reflection**: Write about a challenging experience and how you grew from it.

Please focus on your developed strengths and how they contribute to your resilience.

## Techniques for Ongoing Personal Reflection

- **Weekly Check-Ins:** Set aside time each week to reflect on your experiences, progress, and challenges. Use this time to adjust your practices and set new intentions for the coming week.
- **Mindful Moments:** Incorporate short mindfulness breaks throughout your day to stay connected with your inner self and maintain a sense of joy.
- **Community Sharing:** Share your reflections and experiences with a trusted friend or support group. Engaging in meaningful conversations can deepen your understanding and provide additional insights.

Learning from others' experiences and reflecting on your journey are potent tools for cultivating joy in your daily life. By applying the lessons from real-life examples and engaging in reflective practices, you can discover new ways to integrate joy into your routine and overcome challenges with resilience and positivity. In the next chapter, we will explore the broader impact of joy on the world and how living joyfully can influence and inspire those around you.

# 8 THE BIGGER PICTURE

"Joy is the infallible sign of the presence of God." – Pierre Teilhard de Chardin.

While cultivating joy in our personal lives is vital, its influence extends far beyond the individual. Joy profoundly impacts the broader community and can create a positive ripple effect that touches many lives. This chapter explores the broader implications of personal joy, the ripple effect of joyful living, and how we can envision and commit to a joyful future. By understanding and embracing the bigger picture, we can amplify the joy we cultivate within ourselves and inspire positive change in the world around us.

## 8.1 JOY'S IMPACT ON THE WORLD

Joy is an infectious emotion that naturally radiates outwards, influencing everyone around us. When individuals cultivate joy within themselves, it enhances their relationships with family, friends, and colleagues. A joyful person fosters positive interactions, contributes to a supportive environment, and inspires others. They encourage others to adopt similar attitudes by setting a joyful tone, creating a harmonious and connected society.

**Ripple Effect of Joyful Living:** The ripple effect of joy refers to the phenomenon where one person's joy and positive actions influence others, creating a chain reaction of positivity. Just as a pebble creates ripples when dropped into water, a joyful person can inspire and uplift those around them, leading to a broader impact on the community and beyond. Examples of the Ripple Effect of Joyful Living:

- **A Joyful Teacher:** Teachers who approach their work joyfully can create a positive and inspiring classroom environment, enhancing students' learning experiences and academic success. Their enthusiasm can inspire students to be more engaged, curious, and eager to learn.
- **A Joyful Leader:** A joyful leader in a workplace can boost team morale, increase productivity, and foster a culture of collaboration and innovation. Their positivity can encourage creativity, problem-solving, and a willingness to take risks.
- **A Joyful Parent:** A parent who prioritizes joy can create a nurturing and supportive home environment, positively influencing their children's development and well-being. This joyful atmosphere helps children grow up feeling secure, loved, and motivated to pursue their happiness.

**Real-Life Examples of the Ripple Effect:**

- **Anna's Random Acts of Kindness:** Anna started a personal project of performing random acts of kindness, such as leaving positive notes for strangers or buying coffee for the person behind her in line. Her actions inspired others to do the same, creating a wave of kindness and joy in her community.
- **James's Gratitude Circles:** James initiated gratitude circles in his workplace, where colleagues shared what they were grateful for each week. This practice fostered a culture of appreciation and positivity, improving team dynamics and overall workplace happiness.
- **Sophia's Joyful Parenting:** Sophia's focus on joyful parenting, emphasizing playfulness, gratitude, and mindfulness with her children, not only improved her family's well-being but also influenced other parents in her community to adopt similar practices, creating a more supportive and joyful parenting network.

**Stories of Positive Impact Through Personal Joy:**

- **Rachel's Community Garden Project:** Rachel, who found joy in gardening, started a community garden in her neighborhood. Her enthusiasm and dedication united neighbors, fostering community and shared purpose. The garden became a place for connection, learning, and mutual support, enriching the lives of everyone involved.

- **Michael's Workplace Wellness Initiative:** A corporate manager, Michael introduced wellness programs inspired by his journey to find joy through mindfulness and fitness. His initiatives, including yoga classes and mental health workshops, improved employee well-being and productivity, creating a more positive and supportive work environment.

- **Linda's Volunteer Work with Youth:** Linda, a retiree who found joy in mentoring, started volunteering at a local youth center. Her positive attitude and genuine care for the young people she worked with had a significant impact, helping them build confidence, develop skills, and find their sources of joy.

Joy is contagious; when we express it, we naturally attract and influence others. Our positive emotions strengthen social bonds, increase empathy, and inspire others to spread joy through kindness and gratitude.

## 8.2 Creating a Joyful Future

Creating a joyful future involves envisioning what brings you happiness and taking concrete steps to turn that vision into reality. By engaging in visioning exercises and committing to joy, you can create a life rich in fulfillment and purpose. Visioning exercises help clarify your aspirations and set the foundation for a joyful future. They encourage you to visualize your ideal life and plan how to achieve it.

**Techniques to Envision a Joyful Future:**

- **Guided Visualization:** Spend some quiet time closing your eyes and imagining your ideal future. Picture the relationships, careers, hobbies, and personal growth activities that bring you joy. Imagine yourself living this joyful and fulfilling life, feeling the emotions and experiencing the successes you desire.
- **Future Self Journaling:** Write a letter to your future self describing your joyful future. Include details about your achievements, the people in your life, and the daily practices that sustain your joy. This exercise helps you articulate your vision and serves as a motivational reminder.

**Activities for Creating a Vision Board:**

- **Collect Inspirational Images and Quotes:** Gather images, quotes, and symbols representing your vision of a joyful future. These can include pictures of places you want to visit, activities you enjoy, and inspiring words. Collect items that resonate with your goals and dreams.
- **Assemble Your Vision Board:** Arrange the collected items on a board or digital platform to represent your joyful future visually. Place the vision board somewhere you can see it regularly to remind yourself of your goals and aspirations. This visual tool can help keep you focused and motivated.

**Examples of Successful Visioning:**

- **Claire's Career Transformation:** Claire used visioning exercises to transition from a job she disliked to a fulfilling career in environmental conservation. Her vision board helped her stay focused on her goals and motivated her to take the necessary steps to achieve them, leading to a more satisfying career path.
- **Tom's Personal Growth Journey:** Tom created a vision board focusing on personal growth and wellness. This practice guided him to adopt healthier habits, improve his mental health,

and build meaningful relationships, leading to a more joyful and balanced life.

- **Elena's Community Impact:** Elena envisioned creating a supportive community for single parents. Her vision board included images of community events and support groups. Over time, she successfully established a network that provided resources, support, and joy to many families.

**Commitments to Joy:** Making and keeping commitments to joy involves setting clear goals and consistently taking actions that align with those goals. It requires intentionality and dedication to cultivating joy in daily life. Steps to Make and Keep Commitments to Joy:

- **Set Clear and Achievable Goals:** Define specific goals for cultivating joy, such as daily gratitude practice, regular exercise, or spending quality time with loved ones. Clear goals provide direction and motivation.
- **Create an Action Plan:** Outline the steps needed to achieve your goals, including timelines, resources, and potential challenges. Break down larger goals into smaller, manageable tasks to make them more achievable.

- **Track Your Progress:** Review your goals and action plan regularly. Celebrate your achievements and adjust your approach as needed to stay on track. Tracking progress helps maintain focus and motivation.

**How to Integrate Commitments into Daily Life:**

- **Daily Rituals:** Incorporate joyful practices into your daily routine, such as morning meditation, evening reflection, or regular physical activity. Rituals create consistency and make joy a habitual part of your life.
- **Mindful Living:** Practice mindfulness throughout the day, staying present and fully engaged in your activities. This can enhance your appreciation for the small moments of joy and increase your overall sense of fulfillment.
- **Accountability Partners:** Share your commitments with a trusted friend or family member who can support and encourage you. Regular check-ins can help you stay motivated and accountable, providing a sense of community and shared purpose.

**Long-Term Strategies for Sustaining Joy:**

- **Continuous Learning and Growth:** Stay curious and open to new experiences that bring joy. Pursue hobbies, learn new skills, and seek personal and professional development opportunities. Growth fosters joy and keeps life engaging.
- **Self-Care and Well-Being:** Prioritize self-care practices that nurture physical, mental, and emotional health. This includes proper nutrition, adequate rest, and activities that recharge you. Taking care of yourself is essential for sustained joy.
- **Community Involvement:** Engage in community activities and service projects that align with your values. Building connections and contributing to the well-being of others can enhance your sense of joy and fulfillment, creating a ripple effect of positivity.

Joy can transform our lives and the world around us. We can positively impact our communities by embracing its ripple effect and committing to practices that sustain it. As you cultivate joy, remember that your actions can inspire others, contributing to a more joyful and connected world. Let's commit to spreading joy wherever we go.

# 9 Conclusion

"Joy is the holy fire that keeps our purpose warm and our intelligence aglow." – Helen Keller.

As we end this journey, reflecting on the key takeaways and considering how to continue moving forward with joy is essential. By integrating the insights and practices from each chapter, you can cultivate a life filled with lasting happiness and fulfillment. This conclusion will recap the main points, highlight the most important lessons, and provide encouragement and resources for your continued journey toward joy.

## 9.1 Summarizing Key Takeaways

Here are the Chapter's key takeaways.

1. **The Importance of Joy:** We explored how joy is a fundamental human experience beyond fleeting happiness. Joy profoundly benefits our mental and physical health and significantly enhances our overall well-being and productivity.
2. **Understanding Joy:** We delved into the differences between joy and happiness, the emotional aspects of joy, and the scientific benefits of joy. Understanding these distinctions helps us appreciate the depth and significance of cultivating joy in our lives.

3. **Discovering Contentment:** Contentment is a state of inner peace and satisfaction. We discussed the definition of contentment, how it differs from complacency, and various practices to cultivate contentment, such as mindfulness, gratitude, and acceptance.
4. **Finding Inner Peace:** Inner peace is essential for sustaining joy. This chapter provided techniques to achieve and maintain inner peace, including meditation, creating a peaceful environment, and managing stress and anxiety.
5. **Defining Your Purpose:** Purpose enhances joy and fulfillment. We explored the importance of purpose and how to discover it through self-reflection and by setting meaningful goals aligned with your purpose.
6. **Embracing Personal Growth:** Personal growth is a lifelong journey that enriches our lives. We discussed the principles of a growth mindset, the benefits of personal development, and practical strategies for continuous learning, seeking feedback, and overcoming the fear of failure.
7. **Integrating Joy into Daily Life:** Integrating joy into daily life involves establishing joyful morning routines, finding joy in small moments,

and building joyful habits. We also explored maintaining joy during challenging times through resilience, positive thinking, and support systems.

8. **Case Studies and Personal Stories:** Real-life examples and personal stories provided valuable insights into finding and sustaining joy. We learned from others' experiences and discussed practical steps and reflective exercises to apply these lessons to our lives.

9. **The Bigger Picture:** Joy has a ripple effect that extends beyond the individual. We explored how personal joy influences broader communities and the importance of envisioning and committing to a joyful future. We also discussed the role of supportive relationships and community involvement in maintaining joy.

## 9.2 HIGHLIGHTS OF THE MOST IMPORTANT LESSONS

- Joy is a profound and enduring state that can be cultivated through intentional practices.
- Understanding and differentiating joy and happiness is crucial for long-term well-being.
- Mindfulness, gratitude, and acceptance are vital to discovering contentment and inner peace.

- Having a clear sense of purpose enhances joy and provides direction and motivation.
- Personal growth through a growth mindset, continuous learning, and resilience is essential for a fulfilling life.
- Joy can be integrated into daily life through tiny, consistent practices and building supportive relationships.
- The ripple effect of joy highlights the importance of spreading positivity and making a broader impact on our communities.

As you continue your journey toward joy, revisit the chapters and reflect on the insights and exercises, adapting them as needed. Keep a journal to track your progress and maintain a joyful mindset. Cultivating joy is a lifelong practice that requires dedication. By integrating the practices from this book, you can build a foundation for lasting happiness. Remember, joy is a way of living—embrace the journey, stay open to new experiences, and prioritize joy. Your efforts will enhance your well-being and inspire others. Thank you for joining me on this journey. May your life be filled with happiness and fulfillment.

# 10 Appendices

"Keep your face always toward the sunshine—and shadows will fall behind you." – Walt Whitman.

The "Daily Joy" appendices offer additional resources and tools to help you deepen your practice of cultivating joy. From daily journaling templates to recommended readings and community support options, these appendices are designed to provide ongoing guidance and inspiration as you continue your journey toward lasting happiness and fulfillment.

## 10.1 Daily Joy Journal Templates
### Daily Gratitude Template

- Today, I am grateful for:

    1. _____
    2. _____
    3. _____

- How these things made me feel:

    - _____

- Reflect on a joyful moment today:

    - _____

- What did I learn from today's experiences?

- _____

    How can I create more joy tomorrow?

- _____

## Weekly Reflection Template

- Highlights of the week:

    - _____

- Challenges faced:

    - _____

- Lessons learned:

    - _____

- Moments of joy:

    - _____

- Goals for next week:

    - _____

## Instructions and Tips for Effective Journaling

- **Set a Regular Time:** Choose a specific time each day to journal, such as in the morning or before bed. Consistency helps build a habit.

- **Be Honest and Authentic:** Write openly and honestly about your thoughts and feelings. This is a space for self-reflection and growth.
- **Stay Positive:** Focus on positive experiences and emotions. Even when reflecting on challenges, look for lessons and opportunities for growth.
- **Use Prompts:** If you feel stuck, use prompts like "What brought me joy today?" or "What am I looking forward to tomorrow?"

## 10.2 RECOMMENDED READING AND RESOURCES
### List of Recommended Books

- "The Art of Happiness" by Dalai Lama and Howard Cutler: This book combines the Dalai Lama's teachings on happiness with insights from psychiatrist Howard Cutler. It explores the nature of happiness and provides practical advice for cultivating joy.
- "The Happiness Project" by Gretchen Rubin: Rubin shares her year-long journey of testing various happiness theories and practices in this book. It offers many practical tips and reflections on finding joy in everyday life.
- "The Book of Joy" by Dalai Lama and Desmond Tutu: In this uplifting book, the Dalai Lama and Archbishop Desmond Tutu discuss the nature of

joy and share their wisdom on cultivating it despite life's inevitable challenges.

- "Man's Search for Meaning" by Viktor E. Frankl: Psychiatrist Viktor Frankl reflects on his experiences in Nazi concentration camps and presents his theory of logotherapy, emphasizing the importance of finding meaning and purpose in life as a pathway to joy.
- "The Power of Now" by Eckhart Tolle: This spiritual classic teaches the importance of living in the present moment and offers practical advice on achieving inner peace and joy through mindfulness and presence.

Each recommended book provides unique insights into the nature of joy and practical strategies for cultivating it. They cover various topics, from happiness theories, personal experiences, and spiritual teachings to scientific research on well-being.

**Online Resources and Websites**

- **Coursera:** Offers online courses on happiness, mindfulness, and personal growth from top universities and institutions.
- **Udemy:** Provides a variety of courses on joy, well-being, and self-improvement.

- **Headspace:** A mindfulness app with guided meditations, courses, and resources to help you cultivate joy and reduce stress.
- **Calm** is an app designed to help you practice mindfulness and improve your mental well-being through meditation, sleep stories, and relaxation techniques.

## List of Online and Offline Support Communities

- **Meetup** is a platform where you can find local groups and events based on your interests, such as meditation, book clubs, or hiking groups.
- **Facebook Groups:** Many are dedicated to happiness, mindfulness, and self-improvement topics. Join these groups to connect with like-minded individuals and participate in discussions and events.
- **Local Community Centers:** Check your local community center for classes, workshops, and support groups related to wellness and personal growth.

## Tips for Building Your Support Network

- **Identify Your Needs:** Determine what kind of support you need, whether it's emotional support, accountability, or shared activities.

- **Reach Out:** Don't be afraid to contact friends, family, and colleagues who share your interests. Invite them to join you in activities that bring you joy.
- **Be Open and Inclusive:** Create a welcoming environment for others to join your support network. Encourage open communication and mutual support.
- **Regular Check-Ins:** Schedule regular check-ins with your support network to stay connected and provide encouragement. This can be through in-person meetups, phone calls, or virtual meetings.

The appendices provide additional resources and practical tools to support your journey toward daily joy. You can deepen your understanding and sustain your practices using journal templates, exploring recommended readings, and engaging with supportive communities. Remember, joy is a continuous journey; these resources are here to help you. Embrace the journey, stay curious, and spread joy wherever you go. Thank you for taking this journey with me, and may your life be filled with endless moments of happiness and fulfillment.

## GRATITUDE AND ACKNOWLEDGEMENTS

> "Gratitude is not only the greatest of virtues but the parent of all others." – Cicero.

As I conclude this book, I am deeply grateful to all who have supported, inspired, and encouraged me on this writing journey. Your contributions have been invaluable, and I truly cherish your presence in my life.

To my family, your unwavering support and patience have been instrumental—thank you for believing in me.

I also want to thank my mentors and advisors for their guidance and feedback, which shaped this book.

Your curiosity and commitment to cultivating joy inspire my readers, and I hope this book supports your journey toward lasting happiness.

I am deeply grateful to all who have supported and inspired me. May we continue to spread gratitude and joy together. Thank you for being part of this journey.

## YOUR FEEDBACK MATTERS

"Happiness is not something ready-made. It comes from your actions." – Dalai Lama.

Thank you for reading "Daily Joy: Discover Contentment, Peace, Purpose, and Growth for a Happiness Journey." Your feedback is invaluable and plays a crucial role in enhancing future editions of this book. Please take a moment to answer the following questions:

1. How did this book impact your daily understanding and practice of cultivating joy?
2. Which chapters or sections resonated most with you, and why?
3. Were there any topics or practices you found particularly challenging to implement? How could these be made more accessible?
4. What additional topics or areas would you like to see explored in future editions?
5. How has your perspective on contentment, inner peace, or purpose changed after reading this book?
6. Would you recommend this book to others? If so, why?

Please email your feedback to patildilip23@gmail.com. I read every email and appreciate your time and effort in sharing your thoughts.

Connect with me on Twitter, LinkedIn, or Facebook. Share your insights and experiences using the hashtag #DailyJoy. Engaging with fellow readers can provide additional perspectives and encouragement.

Your insights are greatly appreciated and will significantly contribute to this series's continued growth and development. Thank you for generously sharing your thoughts and experiences!

# About the Author

Dilip Patil is an IT professional with thirty years of experience managing multiple projects across various teams. This experience has enhanced his skills in leadership, strategy, and innovation. His career is marked by a commitment to continuous learning and adaptability, driven by a passion for fostering organizational growth.

Alongside his IT career, Dilip has authored 23 books centered on personal and professional growth, including popular series such as "LEADERSHIP TRANSFORMED," "THE ART OF SUCCESS," and "PROCRASTINATION TRIUMPH," all available on Amazon. His writing journey reflects his dedication to sharing knowledge and inspiring others to reach their full potential.

Writing about joy has become a central theme in Dilip's work, stemming from his belief that joy is foundational to a fulfilling life. This powerful force is more than an emotion; it's a way of living. Through his books, Dilip offers practical strategies to embrace joy amidst the complexities of life, aiming to guide readers on a transformative journey of personal growth.

Dilip's exploration into joy and mindfulness began during his search for balance beyond professional success, leading him to practices that significantly enhanced his well-being. Sharing these insights has enriched his connection with readers who seek similar fulfillment.

Engaging with readers and hearing their stories fuels Dilip's passion for writing and exploration. He invites readers to join him in this ongoing journey to discover and cultivate joy.

https://www.facebook.com/dilip.patil.3979

https://www.linkedin.com/in/dilip-patil-4066a518

https://www.instagram.com/dilip.patil.3979

Thank you for engaging with my work. I want to inspire you to choose joy and pursue a profoundly satisfying life. Let's embrace this journey together.

# Explore More Books

"The journey of a thousand miles begins with one step." – Lao Tzu.

Thank you for reading "Daily Joy: Discover Contentment, Peace, Purpose, and Growth for a Happiness Journey," the first book of the "HAPPINESS JOURNEY." series. If you found value in this book and are eager to continue your personal and professional growth journey, many more resources are available to support you. Explore the following books by Dilip Patil, each offering unique insights and practical strategies to help you achieve your goals.

Through his other esteemed book series, **"THE ART OF SUCCESS," "PROCRASTINATION TRIUMPH," and "LEADERSHIP TRANSFORMED,"** he delves into varied personal and professional growth facets. Each series offers a unique perspective on mastering life's challenges and seizing opportunities for success.

PROCRASTINATION TRIUMPH SERIES

1. Achieve It Now: **An essential guide to overcoming procrastination and improving the future is Beat Procrastination for a Brighter Tomorrow.

2. Temporal Triumph: Defeat Procrastination, Embrace Time Mastery, and Achieve Your Destiny.
3. Action Accelerator: Practical Strategies to Eliminate Procrastination, Propel Your Life and Career Forward.
4. Pathway Pioneer: Overcome Procrastination Through Strategic Habit and Build for Lasting Growth.
5. Success Sculptor: Crafting Habits, Conquering Procrastination, Achieving Goals, and Creating a Path to Enduring Success.

THE ART OF SUCCESS SERIES

1. Empowering Yourself to Achieve Success: This title empowers you to cultivate a mindset conducive to success and fulfillment. It guides you on a transformative exploration of personal development guided by core principles, actionable strategies, and inspiring anecdotes.
2. The Path to Lasting Happiness: Discover the keys to enduring happiness, navigating aspects like purpose, mindset, relationships, resilience, and more. Develop communication finesse, nurture empathy, and acquire skills for multifaceted success.

3. Yoga Flow for Tech Minds: **This title harmonizes ancient wisdom with modern science to enhance productivity, reduce stress, and foster holistic well-being in the digital age. It offers practices tailored for tech minds seeking balance.**
4. The Success Habits: **Delve into the psychology of success to instill winning habits and unlock your full potential. Equip yourself with actionable strategies to elevate your productivity, career, and overall fulfillment.**
5. The Success Mindset: **Discover the secrets to attaining goals and crafting your desired reality. Learn how to nurture a winning mindset, dismantle limiting beliefs, and unleash boundless potential.**
6. Endurance: **Journey deep into enduring and transcending life's tests—an invaluable companion on your path of growth and adaptability.**
7. The Power of Adaptability: **This book complements The Success Formula by exploring adaptability's remarkable influence on shaping destinies.**
8. The Success Formula: **Unlock success and potential with fundamental principles, tools, and**

real-life stories. This guide acts as a compass for personal and professional excellence.

9. Discover the Power of Gratitude: Explore the transformative power of gratitude in personal and professional growth.
10. 10 Pillars of Personal Growth: Embrace resilience, Foster Connections, Cultivate Well-being, and Reach the Zenith of Success.

## LEADERSHIP TRANSFORMED

1. Leadership Awakening: Ignite Self-Awareness, Build Confidence, Foster Growth, And Embark on Your Leadership Journey
2. Visionary Pathways: Unleash Creativity, Foster Resilience, Amplify Impact, and Master Transformational Leadership
3. Masterful Communication: Enhance Influence, Improve Relationships, Boost Persuasion and Transform Leadership Skills
4. Decision Dynamics: Navigate Complexity, Solve Problems, Cultivate Impact, and Empower Leadership through Strategy
5. Empathy & Empowerment: Connect Deeply, Empower Others, Build Trust, and Create Resonant Leadership

6. Innovative Edge: Foster Creativity, Lead Change, Embrace Challenges, and Shape Modern Leadership
7. Resilient Resolve: Overcome Adversity, Maintain Focus, Cultivate Grit, and Build Unstoppable Leadership
8. Legacy Creation: Influence Generations, Achieve Goals, Transform Lives, and Elevate Your Leadership Impact

Each book in the series builds on the last, providing a complete arsenal for personal and professional success. To explore these titles further and for purchasing information, please visit https://www.amazon.com/author/patildilip.

## YOUR GIFT: "THE SUCCESS FORMULA"

The Success Formula complements the principles explored in "Daily Joy: Discover Contentment, Peace, Purpose, and Growth for a Happiness Journey" by providing actionable steps to achieve your goals and enhance your life. To download your free copy, click the link below or scan the QR code:

This eBook is my way of saying thank you and supporting you in your journey toward success and happiness.

www.ingramcontent.com/pod-product-compliance
Lightning Source LLC
Chambersburg PA
CBHW071059240526
45471CB00016B/2170